The Rosicrucian Chemical Marriage

By Christian Rosenkreuz

Copyright © 2020 Lamp of Trismegistus. All rights reserved. No part of this publication may be reproduced or transmitted in any form or by any means, electronic or mechanical, including photocopying, recording, or by any information storage and retrieval system, without permission in writing from Lamp of Trismegistus. Reviewers may quote brief passages.

ISBN: 978-1-63118-458-1

Esoteric Classics

Other Books in this Series and Related Titles

The Rosicrucian Fama Fraternitatis and Confessio Fraternitatis
by Christian Rosenkreuz (978-1-63118-454-3)

Crystal Vision Through Crystal Gazing by Achad (978-1-63118-455-0)

Magical Essays and Instructions by Florence Farr (978-1-63118-418-5)

The Machinery of the Mind by Dion Fortune (978-1-63118-451-2)

Alchemy in the Nineteenth Century
by Helena P. Blavatsky (978-1-63118-446-8)

History, Analysis and Secret Tradition of the Tarot
by Manly P. Hall, A. E. Waite &c (978-1-63118-445-1)

Plato and Platonism and Related Esoteric Essays
by Helena P. Blavatsky & others (978-1-63118-432-1)

The Gospel of the Nativity of Mary by St. Matthew (978-1-63118-448-2)

The Mysteries of Freemasonry & the Druids
by Albert G. Mackey, Manly P. Hall &c (978-1-63118-444-4)

Freemasonry and the Egyptian Mysteries
by C. W. Leadbeater (978-1-63118-456-7)

Lost Atlantis and the Gods of Antiquity & Plato's History of Atlantis
by Carolus Kiesewetterus &c (978-1-63118-431-4)

The Secrets of Enoch by Enoch (978-1-63118-449-9)

The Kabbalah of Masonry & Related Writings
by W. W. Westcott, Eliphas Levi &c (978-1-63118-453-6)

An Outline of Theosophy by C. W. Leadbeater (978-1-63118-452-9)

Thirty-One Hymns to the Star Goddess by Achad (978-1-63118-422-2)

Audio Versions are also Available on Audible and iTunes

Table of Contents

Introduction…7

Preface…9

Foreword…11

The Chemical Marriage

The First Day…13

The Second Day…15

The Third Day…19

The Fourth Day…23

The Fifth Day…27

The Sixth Day…29

The Seventh Day…35

Postscript…37

INTRODUCTION

The word "esoteric" can be difficult to define. Esotericism in general can be seen less as a system of beliefs and more as a category, which encompasses numerous, different systems of beliefs. It's a bit of juxtaposition, since the word "esoteric" indicates something that few people know about, while the term itself broadly covers numerous philosophies, practices, areas of study and belief systems.

In a greater sense, Esotericism acts as a storehouse for secret knowledge, which is often considered ancient (by *tradition, if not by fact)*, passed down from generation to generation, in private. At various times in history, simply possessing the knowledge of some of these subjects, was considered illegal and a jailable offense, if discovered. This usually included such general topics as Alchemy, Qabalah, Hermeticism, Occultism, Ceremonial Magic, Astrology, Divination, Rosicrucianism and so on. Collectively, these areas of study were often referred to as the esoteric sciences.

Sometimes, the outer garment of a subject isn't esoteric, while what is hidden beneath it, is. As an example, Freemasonry isn't necessarily esoteric by nature (at *least not anymore)*, but certain signs, passwords and handshakes given to the candidate during their initiation, are in fact, esoteric, in the sense that they are hidden from the general public.

Today, in the twenty-first century, such topics are readily available at bookstores across the country, and numerous mainsteam publishers offer beginners guides and coffee-table volumes on many of these subjects, intended for mass appeal. Books like *"The Secret"* have turned previously arcane topics into household knowledge. All that being the case, however, it isn't to say that there still aren't buried secrets to uncover, ancient wisdom being ignored and forgotten mysteries to be explored. In fact, it is often that we are only able to further our own studies by standing on the shoulders of these disappearing giants.

Lamp of Trismegistus is doing its part to help preserve humanity's esoteric history by making some of these classics available to those students who are seeking to unearth the knowledge of these ancient colossi.

So, be sure to check other titles from our *Esoteric Classics* series, as well as our *Occult Fiction, Theosophical Classics, Foundations of Freemasonry, Supernatural Fiction, Paranormal Classics* and our *Christian Apocrypha Series.* You can also download the audio versions of most of these titles from iTunes or Audible, for learning on the go.

PREFACE

The anonymous authorship of this seventeenth century text is frequently attributed to Johann Valentin Andreae. *The Chemical Marriage* is often included as the third of the original manifestos of the mysterious "Fraternity of the Rose Cross" (Rosicrucians); however, it is markedly different from the *Fama Fraternitatis* and *Confessio Fraternitatis* in style and in subject matter.

It is an allegoric romance (story) divided into Seven Days, or Seven Journeys, like we encounter in the Old Testament book of *Genesis*, and recounts how a man named Christian Rosenkreuz was invited to go to a wonderful castle full of miracles, in order to assist the Chemical Wedding of the king and the queen, that is, the husband and the bride.

Sometimes titled *The Chymical Wedding* instead, this manifesto has been a source of inspiration for poets, alchemists (the word "chymical" is an old form of "chemical" and refers to alchemy—for which the 'Sacred Marriage' was the goal) and dreamers, through the force of its initiation ritual with processions of tests, purifications, death, resurrection, and ascension and also by its symbolism found since the beginning with the invitation to Rosenkreutz to assist this Royal Wedding.

There is some resemblance between this alchemical romance and passages in the Bible such as: *The kingdom of heaven is like unto a certain king, which made a marriage for his son*, and *And when the king came in to see the guests, he saw there a man which had not on a wedding garment.*[1]

Another biblical reference is: *And I John saw the holy city, new Jerusalem, coming down from God out of heaven, prepared as a bride adorned for her husband.*[2]

What follows is a condensed and modernized version of The Chemical Marriage, told in considerably less veiled language than the original, in an attempt to aid the reader in understanding and following along. So, if at any point you find yourself overwhelmed or confused with the allegory of the story, just remember than the original manuscript, which dates to the early seventeenth century,[3] is much more muddled with symbology.

---

[1] Matthew: 22:2,11
[2] Revelation: 21:2
[3] Sometime between 1601-1616

FOREWORD

The self-admitted author of *The Chemical Marriage*, Johann Valentin Andreæ, born in Württemberg in 1586, was twenty-eight years of age when that work was first published[4]. It was presumably written about twelve years prior to its publication--or when the author was fifteen or sixteen years old. The fact is almost incredible that one so young could produce a volume containing the wealth of symbolic thought and philosophy hidden between the lines of *The Chemical Marriage*. This book makes the earliest known reference to Christian Rosenkreuz, and is generally regarded as the third of the series of original Rosicrucian manifestoes. As a symbolic work, the book itself is hopelessly irreconcilable with the statements made by Andreæ concerning it. The story of *The Chemical Marriage* relates in detail a series of incidents occurring to an aged man, presumably the Father C.R.C. of the *Fama* and *Confessio*. If Father C.R.C. was born in 1378, as stated in the *Confessio*, and is identical with the Christian Rosenkreuz of *The Chemical Marriage*, he was elevated to the dignity of a Knight of the Golden Stone in the eighty-first year of his life (1459). In the light of his own statements, it is inconceivable that Andreæ could have been Father Rosy Cross.

Many figures found in the various books on symbolism published in the early part of the seventeenth century bear a striking resemblance to the characters and episodes in *The*

---

[4] *Although he is the technical author of the present work, it is through the esoteric oral tradition that we have assigned the authorship of this edition to Father C.R.C. himself, in an mystical autobiographical manner.*

Chemical Marriage. The alchemical wedding may prove to be the key to the riddle of Baconian Rosicrucianism. The presence in the German text of *The Chemical Marriage* of some words in English indicates its author to have been conversant also with that language. The following summary of the main episodes of the seven days of *The Chemical Marriage* will give the reader a fairly comprehensive idea of the profundity of its symbolism.

THE CHEMICAL MARRIAGE

THE FIRST DAY

Christian Rosenkreuz, having prepared in his heart the Paschal Lamb together with a small unleavened loaf, was disturbed while at prayer one evening before Easter by a violent storm which threatened to demolish not only his little house but the very hill on which it stood. In the midst of the tempest he was touched on the back and, turning, he beheld a glorious woman with wings filled with eyes, and robed in sky-colored garments spangled with stars. In one hand she held a trumpet and in the other a bundle of letters in every language. Handing a letter to C.R.C.[5], she immediately ascended into the air, at the same time blowing upon her trumpet a blast which shook the house. Upon the seal of the letter was a curious cross and the words *In hoc signo vinces*[6]. Within, traced in letters of gold on an azure field, was an invitation to a royal wedding.

C.R.C. was deeply moved by the invitation because it was the fulfillment of a prophecy which he had received seven years before, but so unworthy did he feel that he was paralyzed with fear. At length, after resorting to prayer, he sought sleep. In his dreams he found himself in a loathsome dungeon with a multitude of other men, all bound and fettered with great chains. The grievousness of their sufferings was increased as they stumbled over each other in the darkness. Suddenly from above came the sound of trumpets; the cover of the dungeon

---

[5] Christian Rosenkreuz
[6] Translated as, "By this sign, you will conquer."

was lifted, and a ray of light pierced the gloom. Framed in the light stood a hoary-headed man who announced that a rope would be lowered seven times and whoever could cling to the rope would be drawn up to freedom.

Great confusion ensued. All sought to grasp the rope and many were pulled away from it by others. C.R.C. despaired of being saved, but suddenly the rope swung towards him and, grasping it, he was raised from the dungeon. An aged woman called the "Ancient Matron" wrote in a golden yellow book the names of those drawn forth, and each of the redeemed was given for remembrance a piece of gold bearing the symbol of the sun and the letters D, L and S.[7] C.R.C., who had been injured while clinging to the rope, found it difficult to walk. The aged woman bade him not to worry, but to thank God who had permitted him to come into so high a light. Thereupon trumpets sounded and C.R.C. awoke, but so vivid was the dream that he was still sensible of the wounds received while asleep.

With renewed faith C.R.C. arose and prepared himself for the *Hermetic Marriage*. He donned a white linen coat and bound a red ribbon crosswise over his shoulders. In his hat he stuck four roses and for food he carried bread, water, and salt. Before leaving his cottage, he knelt and vowed that whatever knowledge was revealed to him he would devote to the service of his neighbor. He then departed from his house with joy.

---

[7] The three letters *D.L.S.* may stand for: "Deus Lux Solis, vel Deo Laus Semper" which can be translated as: "God is the light of the sun" or "Praise to God forever" (also, "Praise always to God").

THE SECOND DAY

As he entered the forest surrounding his little house, it seemed to C.R.C. that all Nature had joyously prepared for the wedding. As he proceeded singing merrily, he came to a green heath in which stood three great cedars, one bearing a tablet with an inscription describing the four paths that led to the palace of the King: the first short and dangerous, the second circuitous, the third a pleasant and royal road, and the fourth suitable only for incorruptible bodies. Weary and perplexed, C.R.C. decided to rest and, cutting a slice of bread, was about to partake thereof when a white dove begged it from him. The dove was at once attacked by a raven, and in his efforts to separate the birds C.R.C. unknowingly ran a considerable distance along one of the four paths--that leading southward. A terrific wind preventing him from retracing his steps, the wedding guest resigned himself to the loss of his bread and continued along the road until he espied in the distance a great gate. The sun being low, he hastened towards the portal, upon which, among other figures, was a tablet bearing the words *Procul hinc procul ite profani*[8].

A gatekeeper in sky-colored habit immediately asked C.R.C. for his letter of invitation and, on receiving it, bade him enter and requested that he purchase a token. After describing himself as a Brother of the Red Rosie Cross, C.R.C. received in exchange for his water bottle a golden disk bearing the letters

---

[8] This may be translated as, "Go far away from here, you profane ones!"

S and C.⁹ Night drawing near, the wanderer hastened on to a second gate, guarded by a lion, and to which was affixed a tablet with the words *Date et dabitur volis*¹⁰, where he presented a letter given him by the first gatekeeper. Being urged to purchase a token bearing the letters S M,¹¹ he gave his little package of salt and then hastened on to reach the palace gates before they were locked for the night.

A beautiful virgin called *Virgo Lucifera* was extinguishing the castle lights as C.R.C. approached, and he was barely able to squeeze through the closing gates. As they closed they caught part of his coat, which he was forced to leave behind. Here his name was written in the Lord Bridegroom's little vellum book and he was presented with a new pair of shoes and also a token bearing the letters S, P and N.¹² He was then conducted by pages to a small chamber where the "ice-grey locks" were cut from the crown of his head by invisible barbers, after which he was ushered into a spacious hall where a goodly number of kings, princes, and commoners were assembled. At the sound of trumpets each seated himself at the table, taking a position corresponding to his dignity, so that C.R.C. received a very humble seat. Most of the pseudo-philosophers present being vain pretenders, the banquet became an orgy, which, however, suddenly ceased at the sound of stately and inspired

---

⁹ The two letters *S.C.* may stand for: *"Sanctitate Constantia. Sponsus Charus. Spes Caritas"* which can be translated as: *"Constancy by holiness. Beloved bridegroom. Hope, Charity."*

¹⁰ Translated as, "Give and it shall be given to you" (Luke: 6:38)

¹¹ The two letters *S.M.* may stand for: *"Studio merentis. Sponso mittendus. Sal Mineralis. Sal Menstrualis"* which can be translated as: *"By the study of a deserving man. To be given to the bridegroom. Mineral salt. Menstral salt."*

¹² The letters *S.P.N.* may stand for: *"Sponsi praesentandus nuptiis. Salus per naturam"* which can be translated as: *"To be given at the bridegroom's wedding. Healing through nature. (Also, Salvation through nature)"*

Chymische Hoch-
zeit:
Christiani Rosencreutz.
ANNO 1459.

Arcana publicata vilescunt; & gratiam prophanata amittunt.

Ergo: ne Margaritas objyce porcis, seu Asino substerne rosas.

Straßburg/
In Verlägung / Lazari Zetzners.
Anno M. DC. XVI.

---

[13] The most remarkable of all the publications involved in the Rosicrucian controversy is that of *The Chemical Marriage*, published in Strasbourg. This work, which is very rare, should be reproduced in exact facsimile to provide students with the opportunity of examining the actual text for the various forms of cipher employed. Probably no other volume in the history or literature created such a profound disturbance as this unpretentious little book. Immediately following its publication the purpose for which the volume was intended became the subject of popular speculation. It was both attacked and defended by theologians and philosophers alike, but when the various contending elements are simmered down the mysteries surrounding the book remain unsolved. That its author was a man of exceptional learning was admitted, and it is noteworthy that those minds which possessed the deepest understanding of Nature's mysteries were among those profoundly impressed by the contents of *The Chemical Marriage*.

music. For nearly half an hour no one spoke. Then amidst a great sound the door of the dining hall swung open and thousands of lighted tapers held by invisible hands entered. these were followed by the two pages lighting the beautiful *Virgo Lucifera* seated on a self-moving throne. The white-and-gold-robed Virgin then rose and announced that to prevent the admission of unworthy persons to the mystical wedding a set of scales would be erected the following day upon which each guest would be weighed to determine his integrity. Those unwilling to undergo this ordeal she stated should remain in the dining hall. She then withdrew, but many of the tapers stayed to accompany the guests to their quarters for the night.

Most of those present were presumptuous enough to believe that they could be safety weighed, but nine--including C.R.C.--felt their shortcomings so deeply that they feared the outcome and remained in the hall while the others were led away to their sleeping chambers. These nine were bound with ropes and left alone in darkness. C.R.C. then dreamed that he saw many men suspended over the earth by threads, and among them flew an aged man who, cutting here and there a thread, caused many to fall to earth. Those who in arrogance had soared to lofty heights accordingly fell a greater distance and sustained more serious injury than the more humble ones who, falling but a short distance, often landed without mishap. Considering this dream to be a good omen, C.R.C. related it to a companion, continuing in discourse with him until dawn.

THE THIRD DAY

Soon after dawn the trumpets sounded and the *Virgo Lucifera*, arrayed in red velvet, girded with a white sash, and crowned with a laurel wreath, entered accompanied by two hundred men in red-and- white livery. She intimated to C.R.C. and his eight companions that they might fare better than the other, self-satisfied guests. Golden scales were then hung in the midst of the hall and near them were placed seven weights, one good-sized, four small, and two very large. The men in livery, each carrying a naked sword and a strong rope, were divided into seven groups and from each group was chosen a captain, who was given charge of one of the weights. Having remounted her high throne, *Virgo Lucifera* ordered the ceremony to begin. The first to step on the scales was an emperor so virtuous that the balances did not tip until six weights had been placed upon the opposite end. He was therefore turned over to the sixth group. The rich and poor alike stood upon the scales, but only a few passed the test successfully. To these were given velvet robes and wreaths of laurel, after which they were seated upon the steps of *Virgo Lucifera's* throne. Those who failed were ridiculed and scourged.

The "inquisition" being finished, one of the captains begged *Virgo Lucifera* to permit the nine men who had declared themselves unworthy also to be weighed, and this caused C.R.C. anguish and fear. Of the first seven one succeeded and was greeted with joy. C.R.C. was the eighth and he not only withstood all the weights but even when three men hung on the opposite end of the beam he could not be moved. A page cried out: "THAT IS HE!" C.R.C. was quickly set at liberty and permitted to release one of the captives. He chose the first emperor. *Virgo Lucifera* then requested the red roses that C.R.C. carried, which he immediately gave her. The ceremony of the scales ended about ten o'clock in the forenoon.

After agreeing upon the penalties to be imposed upon those whose shortcomings had been thus exposed, a dinner was served to all. The few successful "artists," including C.R.C., were given the chief seats, after which the Golden Fleece and a Flying Lion were bestowed upon them in the name of the Bridegroom. *Virgo Lucifera* then presented a magnificent goblet to the guests, stating that the King had requested all to share its contents, Following this, C.R.C. and his companions were taken out upon a scaffolding where they beheld the various penalties suffered by those who failed. Before leaving the palace, each of the rejected guests was given a draught of forgetfulness. The elect then returned to the castle, where to each was assigned a learned page, who conducted them through the various parts of the edifice. C.R.C. saw many things his companions were not privileged to behold, including the Royal Sepulcher, where he learned "more than is extant in all books." He also visited a magnificent library and an observatory containing a great globe thirty feet in diameter and with all the countries of the world marked upon it.

At supper the various guests propounded enigmas and C.R.C. solved the riddle which *Virgo Lucifera* asked concerning her own identity. Then entered the dining hall two youths and six virgins beautifully robed, followed by a seventh virgin wearing a coronet. The latter was called the Duchess, and was mistaken for the Hermetic Bride. The Duchess told C.R.C. that he had received more than the others, therefore should make a greater return. The Duchess then asked each of the virgins to pick up one of the seven weights which still remained in the great room. To *Virgo Lucifera* was given the heaviest weight, which was hung in the Queen's chamber during the singing of a hymn. In the second chamber the first virgin hung her weight during a similar ceremony; thus they proceeded from room to room until the weights had been disposed of. The Duchess then presented her hand to C.R.C. and his companions and, followed by her virgins, withdrew. Pages then conducted the guests to their sleeping chambers. The one assigned to C.R.C. was hung with rare tapestries and with beautiful paintings.

THE FOURTH DAY

After washing and drinking in the garden from a fountain which bore several inscriptions--among them one reading, "Drink, brothers, and live"--the guests, led by *Virgo Lucifera*, ascended the 365 steps of the royal winding stairs. The guests were given wreaths of laurel and, a curtain being raised, found themselves in the presence of the King and Queen. C.R.C. was awestruck by the glory of the throne room and especially by the magnificence of the Queen's robes, which were so dazzling that he could not gaze upon them. Each guest was presented to the King by one of the virgins and after this ceremony the *Virgo Lucifera* made a short speech in which she recited the achievements of the honest "artists" and begged that each be questioned as to whether she had properly fulfilled her duty. Old Atlas then stepped forward and in the name of their Royal Majesties greeted the intrepid band of philosophers and assured *Virgo Lucifera* that she should receive a royal reward.

The length of the throne room was five times its width. To the west was a great porch in which stood three thrones, the central one elevated. On each throne sat two persons: on the first an ancient king with a young consort; on the third a black king with a veiled matron beside him; and on the central throne two young persons over whose heads hung a large and costly crown, about which hovered a little Cupid who shot his arrows first at the two lovers and then about the hall. Before the Queen a book bound in black velvet lay on a small altar, on which were golden decorations. Beside this were a burning candle, a celestial globe, a small striking-watch, a little crystal

Here followeth the Figure conteyning all
the secrets of the Treatise both great & small

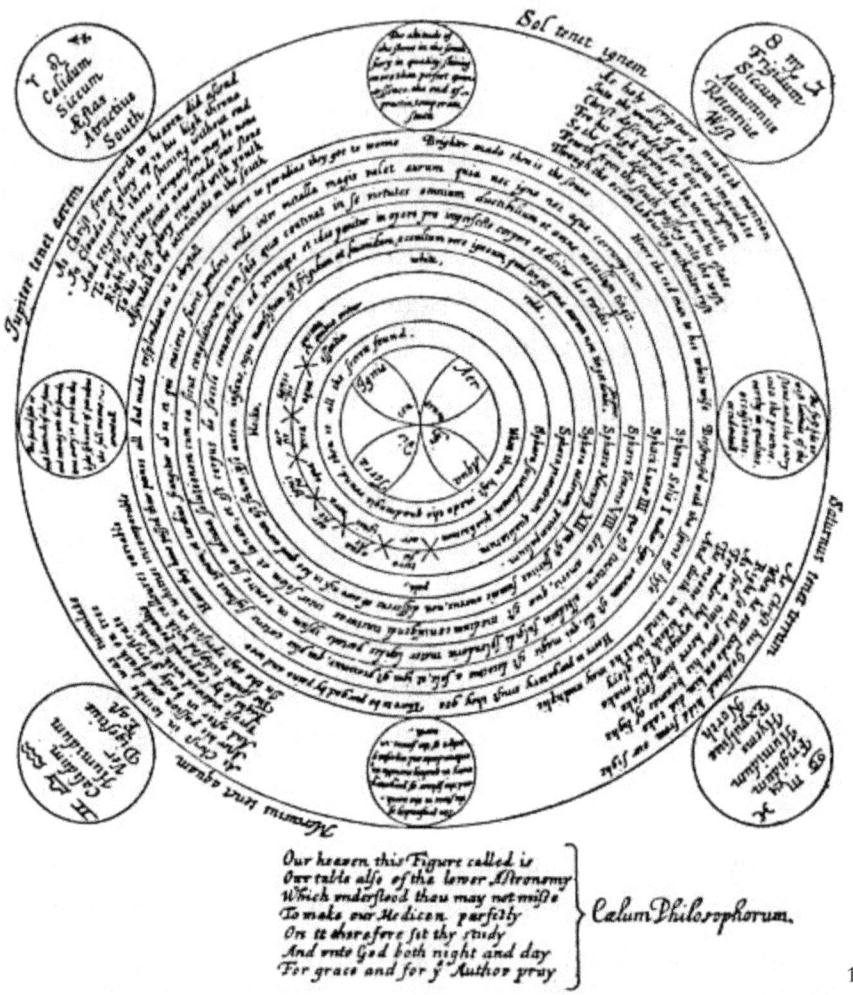

} Cælum Philosophorum.

[14] This plate, which is the key to mystic Christian alchemy, is missing from almost every copy of the *Theatrum Chemicum Britannicum*, a work compiled by Elias Ashmole and containing about a score of pieces by English poets treating of the Philosopher's Stone and the Hermetic mysteries. In view of the consistent manner in which the plate disappeared, it is possible that the diagram was purposely removed because it revealed too plainly the Rosicrucian arcana. Worthy of notice also is the care with which owners' names have been effaced from early books pertaining to alchemy and Hermeticism. The original names are usually rendered illegible being covered with heavy ink lines, the procedure often seriously defacing the volume, While an occasional exception is found, in practically every instance the mutilated books either deal with Rosicrucianism or contain cryptic writings of suspected Rosicrucian origin. It is presumed that this Practice of obliterating the owners names was to

pipe from which ran a stream of clear blood-red liquor, and a skull with a white serpent crawling in and out of the orbits. After their presentations, the guests retired down the winding stairs to the great hall.

Later the *Virgo Lucifera* announced that a comedy was to be performed for the benefit of the six royal guests in a building called the House of the Sun. C.R.C. and his companions formed part of the royal procession, which after a considerable walk arrived at the theater. The play was in seven acts, and after its happy ending all returned through the garden and up the winding stairs to the throne room. C.R.C. noticed the young King was very sad and that at the banquet following he often sent meat to the white serpent in the skull. The feast over, the young King, holding in his hand the little black book from the altar, asked the guests if they would all be true to him through prosperity and adversity, and when they tremblingly agreed he asked that each should sign his name in the little black book as proof of his fealty. The royal persons then drank from the little crystal fountain, the others afterwards doing likewise. This was called the "Draught of Silence." The royal persons then sadly shook hands with all present. Suddenly a little bell tinkled and immediately the kings and queens took off their white garments and donned black ones, the room was hung in sable draperies, and the tables were removed. The eyes of the royal persons were bound with six black taffeta scarfs and six coffins were

---

prevent the early Rosicrucians and Hermetists from being discovered through the volumes composing their libraries. Elias Ashmole's plate shows the analogies between the life of Christ and the four grand divisions of the alchemical process. Herein is also revealed the teaching that the Philosopher's Stone itself is a macrocosm and a microcosm, embodying the principles of astronomy and cosmogony, both universal and human.

placed in the center of the room. An executioner, a Moor, robed in black and bearing an axe, entered, and beheaded in turn each of the six royal persons. The blood of each was caught in a golden goblet, which was placed in the coffins with the body. The executioner was also decapitated and his head placed in a small chest.

The *Virgo Lucifera*, after assuring C.R.C. and his companions that all should be well if they were faithful and true, ordered the pages to conduct them to their rooms for the night while she remained to watch with the dead. About midnight C.R.C. awakened suddenly and, looking from his window, beheld seven ships sailing upon a lake. Above each hovered a flame; these he believed to be the spirits of the beheaded. When the ships reached shore, the *Virgo Lucifera* met them and on each of six of the vessels was placed a covered coffin. As soon as the coffins had been thus disposed of, the lights were extinguished and the flames passed back over the lake so that there remained but one light for a watch in each ship. After beholding this strange ceremony, C.R.C. returned to his bed and slept till morning.

THE FIFTH DAY

Rising at daybreak and entreating his page to show him other treasures of the palace, C.R.C. was conducted down many steps to a great iron door bearing a curious inscription, which he carefully copied. Passing through, he found himself in the royal treasury, the light in which came entirely from some huge carbuncles. In the center stood the triangular sepulcher of Lady Venus. Lifting a copper door in the pavement, the page ushered C.R.C. into a crypt where stood a great bed upon which, when his guide had raised the coverlets, C.R.C. beheld the body of Venus. Led by his page, C.R.C. then rejoined his companions, saying nothing to them of his experience.

Virgo Lucifera, robed in black velvet and accompanied by her virgins, then led the guests out into the courtyard where stood six coffins, each with eight pallbearers. C.R.C. was the only one of the group of "artists" who suspected the royal bodies were no longer in these coffins. The coffins were lowered into graves and great stones rolled over them. The *Virgo Lucifera* then made a short oration in which she exhorted each to assist in restoring the royal persons to life, declaring that they should journey with her to the Tower of Olympus, where the medicines necessary to the resurrection of the six royal persons could alone be found. C.R.C. and his companions followed *Virgo Lucifera* to the seashore, where all embarked on seven ships disposed according to a certain strange order. As the ships sailed across the lake and through a narrow channel into the open sea, they were attended by sirens, nymphs, and sea goddesses, who in honor of the wedding presented a great and beautiful pearl to the royal couple. When the ships came in sight of the Tower of Olympus, *Virgo Lucifera* ordered the discharge of cannon to signal their approach. Immediately a white flag appeared upon the tower and a small gilded pinnace, containing an ancient man--the warden of the tower--with his white-clad guards came out to meet the ships.

    The Tower of Olympus stood upon an island which was exactly square and was surrounded by a great wall. Entering the gate, the group was led to the bottom of the central tower, which contained an excellent laboratory where the guests were fain to beat and wash plants, precious stones, and all sorts of things, extract their juice and essence, and put these latter into glasses. *Virgo Lucifera* set the "artists" to work so arduously that they felt they were mere drudges. When the day's work was finished, each was assigned a mattress on the stone floor. Being unable to sleep, C.R.C. wandered about contemplating the stars. Chancing upon a flight of steps leading to the top of the wall, he climbed up and looked out upon the sea. Remaining here for some time, about midnight he beheld seven flames which, passing over the sea towards him, gathered themselves on the top of the spire of the central tower. Simultaneously the winds arose, the sea became tempestuous, and the moon was covered with clouds. With some fear C.R.C. ran down the stairs and returned to the tower and, lying down on his mattress, was lulled to sleep by the sound of a gently flowing fountain in the laboratory.

THE SIXTH DAY

The next morning the aged warden of the tower, after examining the work performed by the wedding guests in the laboratory and finding it satisfactory, caused ladders, ropes, and large wings to be brought forth, and addressed the assembled "artists" thus: "My dear sons, one of these three things must each of you this day constantly bear about with him." Lots were cast and to C.R.C., much to his chagrin, fell a heavy ladder. Those who secured wings had them fastened to their backs so cunningly that it was impossible to detect that they were artificial. The aged warden then locked the "artists" in the lower room of the tower, but in a short time a round hole was uncovered in the ceiling and *Virgo Lucifera* invited all to ascend. Those with wings flew at once through the opening, those with ropes had many difficulties, while C.R.C. with his ladder made reasonable speed. On the second floor the wedding guests, musicians, and *Virgo Lucifera* gathered about a fountain-like contrivance containing the bodies of the six royal persons.

Virgo Lucifera then placed the if Moor's head in a kettle-like receptacle in the upper part of the fountain and poured upon it the substances prepared on the previous day in the laboratory. The virgins placed lamps beneath. These substances when they boiled passed out through holes in the sides of the kettle and, falling upon the bodies in the fountain below, dissolved them. The six royal bodies having been reduced thus to a liquid state, a tap was opened in the lower end of the fountain and the fluid drained into an immense golden globe, which, when filled, was of great weight. All but the wedding

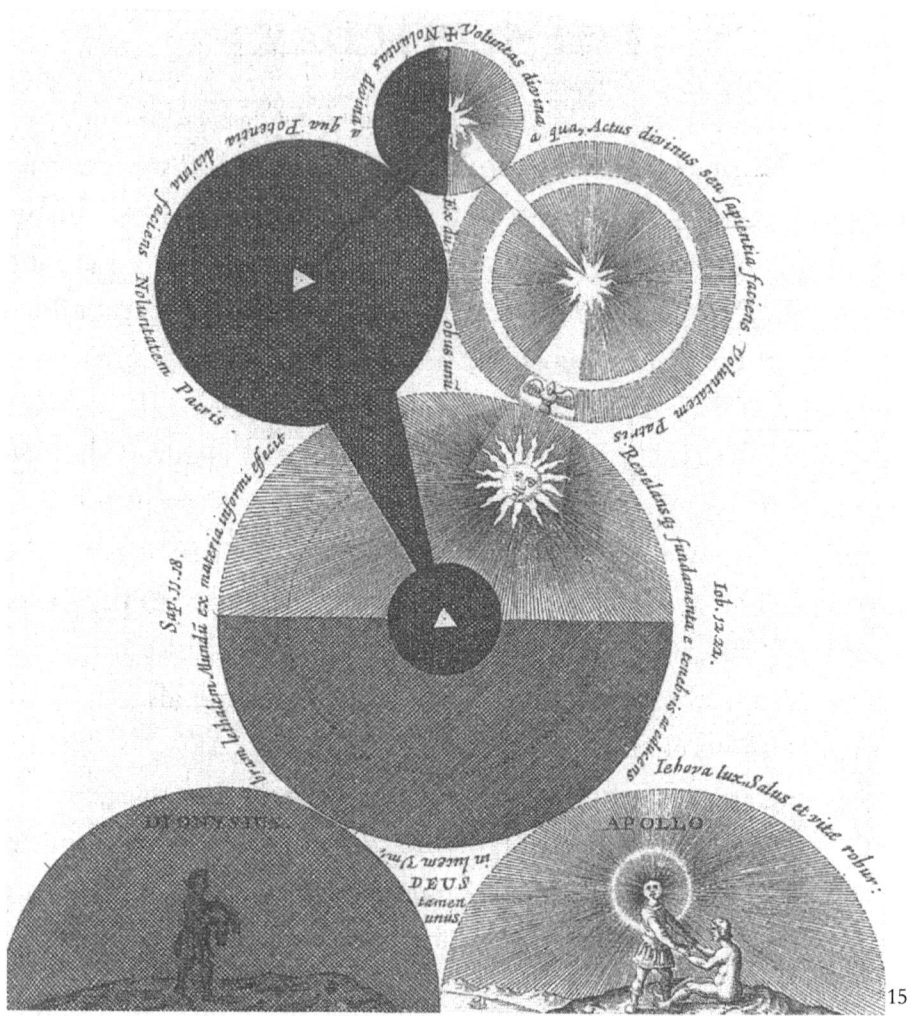

[15] The Supreme Deity is symbolized by the small globe at the top, which is divided into two hemispheres, the dark half representing the divine darkness with which the Deity surround Himself and which serves as His hiding place. The radiant hemisphere signifies the divine light which is in God and which, pouring forth, manifests as the objective creative power. The large dark globe to the left and beneath the dark half of the upper sphere signifies the potential darkness which was upon the face of the primordial deep and within which moved the Spirit of God. The light globe to the right is the Deity who is revealed out of the darkness. Here the shining Word has dissipated the shadows and a glorious universe has been formed. The divine power of this radiant globe is cognizable to man as the sun. The large light and a dark section represents the created universes partaking of the light and darkness which are in the nature of the Creator. The dark half represents the Deep, or Chaos, the Eternal Waters pouring forth out of the Deity; the light half-circle containing the figure of Apollo represents the diurnal hemisphere of the world, which in the ancient Mysteries was ruled over by Apollo. The dark

guests then retired and shortly a hole in the ceiling opened as before and the guests ascended pell-mell to the third floor. Here the globe were suspended by a strong chain. The walls of the apartment were of glass, and mirrors were so arranged that the sun's rays were concentrated upon the central globe, thus causing it to become very hot. Later the sun's rays were deflected and the globe permitted to cool, after which it was cut open with a diamond, revealing a beautiful white egg. Carrying this with her, *Virgo Lucifera* departed.

The guests, having ascended through another trap door, found themselves upon the fourth floor, where stood a square kettle filled with silver sand warmed by a gentle fire. The great white egg was placed upon the warm sand to mature. In a short time it cracked and there emerged an ugly, ill-tempered bird, which was fed with the blood of the beheaded royal persons diluted with prepared water. At each feeding its feathers changed color; from black they turned to white and at last they became varicolored, the disposition of the bird improving the while. Dinner was then served, after which *Virgo Lucifera* departed with the bird. The guests ascended with ropes, ladders, and wings to the fifth floor, where a bath colored with fine white powder had been prepared for the bird, which enjoyed bathing in it until the lamps placed beneath the bath caused the water to become uncomfortably warm. When the heat had removed all the bird's feathers it was taken out, but the fire continued until nothing remained in the bath save a sediment in the form of a blue stone. This was later pounded

---

half-circle is the nocturnal hemisphere ruled over by Dionysius (Dionysos), whose figure is faintly visible in the gloom.

up and made into a pigment; with this, all of the bird except the head was painted.

The guests thereupon ascended to the sixth floor, where stood a small altar resembling that in the King's throne room. The bird drank from the little fountain and was fed with the blood of the white serpent which crawled through the openings in the skull. The sphere by the altar revolved continuously. The watch struck one, two, and then three, at which time the bird, laying its neck upon the book, suffered itself to be decapitated. Its body was burned to ashes, which were placed in a box of cypress wood. *Virgo Lucifera* told C.R.C. and three of his comrades that they were lazy and sluggish "labourators" and would therefore be excluded from the seventh room. Musicians were sent for, who with cornets were to "blow" the four in ridicule from the chamber. C.R.C. and his three companions were disheartened until the musicians told them to be of good cheer and led them up a winding stair to the eighth floor of the tower directly beneath the roof. Here the old warden, standing upon a little round furnace, welcomed them and congratulated them upon being chosen by *Virgo Lucifera*, for this greater work. *Virgo Lucifera* then entered, and after laughing at the perplexity of her guests, emptied the ashes of the bird into another vessel, filling the cypress box with useless matter. She thereupon returned to the seventh floor, presumably to mislead those assembled there by setting them to work upon the false ashes in the box.

C.R.C. and his three friends were set to work moistening the bird's ashes with specially prepared water until the mixture became of dough-like consistency, after which it was heated and molded into two miniature forms. Later these were opened, disclosing two bright and almost transparent human images about four inches high (homunculi), one male and the other female. These tiny forms were laid upon satin cushions and fed drop by drop with the blood of the bird until they grew to normal size and of great beauty. Though the bodies had the consistency of flesh, they showed no signs of life, for the soul was not in them. The bodies were next surrounded with torches and their faces covered with silk. *Virgo Lucifera* then appeared, bearing two curious white garments. The virgins also entered, among them six bearing great trumpets. A trumpet was placed upon the mouth of one of the two figures and C.R.C. saw a tiny hole open in the dome of the tower and a ray of light descend through the tube of the trumpet and enter the body. This process was repeated three times on each body. The two newly ensouled forms were then removed upon a traveling couch. In about half an hour the young King and Queen awakened and the *Virgo Lucifera* presented them with the white garments. These they donned and the King in his own person most graciously returned thanks to C.R.C. and his companions, after which the royal persons departed upon a ship. C.R.C. and his three privileged friends then rejoined the other "artists," making no mention of that which they had seen. Later the entire party were assigned handsome chambers, where they rested till morning.

THE SEVENTH DAY

In the morning *Virgo Lucifera* announced that each of the wedding guests had become a "Knight of the Golden Stone. " The aged warden then presented each man with a gold medal, bearing on one side the inscription "Ar. Nat. Mi."[16] and on the other, "Tem. Na. F."[17] The entire company returned in twelve ships to the King's palace. The flags on the vessels bore the signs of the zodiac, and C.R.C. sat under that of Libra. As they entered the lake, many ships met them and the King and Queen, together with their lords, ladies, and virgins, rode forth on a golden barge to greet the returning guests. Atlas then made a short oration in the King's behalf, also asking for the royal presents. In reply the aged warden delivered to Cupid, who hovered about the royal pair, a small, curious-shaped casket. C.R.C. and the old lord, each bearing a snow-white ensign with a red cross on it, rode in the carriage with the King. At the first gate stood the porter with blue clothes, who, upon seeing C.R.C., begged him to intercede with the King to release him from that post of servitude. The King replied that the porter was a famous astrologer who was forced to keep the gate as a punishment for the crime of having gazed upon Lady Venus reposing upon her couch. The King further declared that the porter could be released only when another was found who had committed the same crime. Upon hearing this, C.R.C.'s heart

---

[16] "*Ars naturae ministra*" which can be translated as: "Art is the priestess *(or: hand-maiden)* of nature."

[17] "*Temporis natura filia*" which can be translated as: "Nature is the daughter of Time"

sank, for he realized himself to be the culprit, but he remained silent at that time.

The newly created Knights of the Golden Stone were obliged to subscribe to five articles drawn up by His Royal Highness: (1) That they would ascribe their Order only to God and His handmaid, Nature. (2) That they should abominate all uncleanness and vice. (3) That they should always be ready to assist the worthy and needy. (4) That they should not use their knowledge and power for the attainment of worldly dignity. (5) That they should not desire to live longer than God had decreed. They were then duly installed as Knights, which ceremony was ratified in a little chapel where C. R. C. hung up his Golden Fleece and his hat for an eternal memorial, and here he inscribed the following: *Summa Scientia nihil Scire. Fr. Christianus Rosenkreuz. Eques aurei Lapidis.*[18] Anno 1459.

After the ceremony, C.R.C. admitted that he was the one who had beheld Venus and consequently must become the porter of the gate. The King embraced him fondly and he was assigned to a great room containing three beds--one for himself, one for the aged lord of the tower, and the third for old Atlas.

---

[18] Translated as, "The Highest Knowledge is to Know Nothing. Brother Christian Rosenkreutz. Knight of the Golden Stone."

POSTSCRIPT

It is at this point in the tale that *The Chemical Marriage* comes to an abrupt end, leaving the impression that C.R.C. was to assume his duties as porter on the following morning. The book ends in the middle of a sentence, with a note in italics presumably by the editor.

Under the symbolism of an alchemical marriage, mediæval philosophers concealed the secret system of spiritual culture whereby they hoped to coordinate the disjecta membra of both the human and social organisms. Society, they maintained, was a threefold structure and had its analogy in the triune constitution of man, for as man consists of spirit, mind, and body, so society is made up of the church, the state, and the populace. The bigotry of the church, the tyranny of the state, and the fury of the mob are the three murderous agencies of society which seek to destroy Truth as recounted in the Masonic legend of Hiram Abiff[19]. The first six days of *The Chemical Marriage* set forth the processes of philosophical "creation" through which every organism must pass. The three kings are the threefold spirit of man and their consorts the corresponding vehicles of their expression in the lower world. The executioner is the mind, the higher part of which--symbolized by the head--is necessary to the achievement of the philosophical labor. Thus the parts of man--by the alchemists symbolized as planets and elements--when blended together according to a certain Divine formula result in the creation of

---

[19] See *The Lost Keys of Freemasonry or The Secret of Hiram Abiff* by Manly P. Hall in our *Foundations of Freemasonry Series*.

two philosophic "babes" which, fed upon the blood of the alchemical bird, become rulers of the world.

From an ethical standpoint, the young King and Queen resurrected at the summit of the tower and ensouled by Divine Life represent the forces of Intelligence and Love which must ultimately guide society. Intelligence and Love are the two great ethical luminaries of the world and correspond to enlightened spirit and regenerated body. The bridegroom is *reality* and the bride the regenerated being who attains perfection by becoming one with reality through a cosmic marriage wherein the mortal part attains immortality by being united with its own immortal Source. In the *Hermetic Marriage* divine and human consciousness are united in holy wedlock and he in whom this sacred ceremony takes place is designated as "Knight of the Golden Stone"; he thereby becomes a divine philosophic diamond composed of the quintessence of his own sevenfold constitution.

Such is the true interpretation of the mystical process of becoming "a bride of the Lamb." The Lamb of God is signified by the Golden Fleece that Jason was forced to win before he could assume his kingship. The Flying Lion is illumined will, an absolute prerequisite to the achievement of the Great Work. The episode of weighing the souls of men has its parallel in the ceremony described in the *Egyptian Book of the Dead*. The walled city entered by C.R.C. represents the sanctuary of wisdom wherein dwell the real rulers of the world--the initiated philosophers.

Like the ancient Mysteries after which it was patterned, the Order of the Rose Cross possessed a secret ritual which was lived by the candidate for a prescribed number of years before he was eligible to the inner degrees of the society. The various floors of the Tower of Olympus represent the orbits of the planets. The ascent of the philosophers from one floor to another also parallels certain rituals of the Eleusinian Mysteries and the rites of Mithras wherein the candidate ascended the seven rungs of a ladder or climbed the seven steps of a pyramid in order to signify release from the influences of the Planetary Governors. Man becomes master of the seven spheres only when he transmutes the impulses received from them. He who masters the seven worlds and is reunited with the Divine Source of his own nature consummates the *Hermetic Marriage*.

www.ingramcontent.com/pod-product-compliance
Lightning Source LLC
LaVergne TN
LVHW041503070426
835507LV00009B/780